Fear Not

JOHN HOUGHTON
AND
DAVE ROBERTS

KINGSWAY PUBLICATIONS
EASTBOURNE

First published 2002

ISBN 1 84291 063 9

Published by
KINGSWAY COMMUNICATIONS LTD
Lottbridge Drove, Eastbourne, BN23 6NT, England.
Email: books@kingsway.co.uk

Book design and production for the publishers by
Bookprint Creative Services, P.O. Box 827, BN21 3YJ, England.
Printed in Great Britain.

Contents

Introduction

A few months ago, while filling in a returned goods form in a car spares store, I – John – got into some light-hearted banter with the checkout girl about the day and the month, when she suddenly blurted out, 'I'm afraid!' When I asked why, she said, 'I've read Nostradamus and he says the world is going to end.' She added later in the conversation, 'I'm afraid of becoming 18, too. I don't think I can cope with the responsibility of being an adult in this world.' I was able to point her to a book that is far more reliable than the dubious writings of Nostradamus, but it brought home to me the need for a compassionate but clear pastoral voice to speak to the worried hearts of men and women.

The world changed for all of us on the 11th September 2001 and the need for that pastoral voice has grown more urgent. Western democracy, complacent under its nuclear umbrella, proved to be terrifyingly vulnerable as highly co-ordinated terrorists turned passenger jets into suicide bombs and killed thousands. On that day, confidence in the new world order – much heralded by President George Bush's father during his term of office – crumbled as a stunned world watched the spectacular destruction of the World Trade Center. The images will haunt all of us for years to come.

I – Dave – had returned home early that Tuesday, exhausted after a 16-hour day on the Monday. My wife, Sharon, told me at the door that something was happening in New York with planes and the World Trade Center. The first attack had happened 20 minutes before. I sat aghast as the tragedy unfolded; my mind a tumult of questions, emotions and fears. The questions were about world politics and Christian witness, the emotion a sense of the desolation many would already be feeling, the fear mainly that the situation was out of control and that another high profile target would be hit soon.

I retreated to my small study for a few minutes, feeling physically sick. Soon I would face the questions that many parents faced that day. 'Is this the end of the world?' 'Will we still be here in the morning?' Before the day was finished I would sit with my two sons, explain to them that everything had changed in our world, but we would be safe tonight and then pray with them and for them.

At 4.00 pm I rang John Houghton, who like myself contributes to the leadership of a local church in Eastbourne on England's south coast. Our senior leader was away on holiday. How should we respond to the tragedies of the previous two hours? We decided to cancel our midweek small groups and call a prayer meeting at the church. We gathered the community of faith together and we talked and prayed. People told us later that this helped them and enabled them to help others. The themes that emerged during that evening form the bedrock for this book.

Like many of our readers, we gathered on the following Sunday, seeking to find a way of expressing both our sorrow and our hope. The words of the Noel Richards/Gerald Coates song 'Great is the Darkness' seemed the most appropriate, with the poetic lament of 'watching while sanity dies' capturing our sense of disbelief, and the surging final verse celebrating Christ's return, expressing the hope that would see us through the darkest of times.

A few weeks later I picked up *Time* magazine with its stark cover headline, 'The Fear Factor'. This was the fear that was sparking the air industry collapse; the soul-searching that brought 800 people to Exeter Cathedral on the 16th September instead of the normal 80; the panic buying of gas masks and the enquiries about boarding schools far from large city centres. What you read in this book reflects our pilgrimage through the landscape of fear that has gripped many, including ourselves. We offer it to you as a practical response to the new world disorder that surrounds us and touches all our lives in both the momentous and the mundane.

Life is no longer as safe as we thought; even the Pentagon, the military heart of the West, was struck. War has been declared, but by an invisible enemy networked on a global scale. Apart from a short-term victory in Afghanistan, there is little confidence that it can be won and it might easily escalate into a mass conflict between Islamic nations and the West. Yet even if that scenario is avoided, the enemy is subversive and calculating. Anthrax spores sent through the post create an air of unpredictability and raise the spectre of insidious biochemical attacks on the civilian population. What other threats await us?

The events of the 11th September are in fact only part of a wider crisis of confidence. Holes in the ozone layer threaten us with cancer. HIV makes sex potentially fatal. E-coli and salmonella outbreaks, to say nothing of the BSE scandal, have reduced confidence in our food supplies to an all-time low. Foot and mouth disease threatens our livestock and restricts our access to the countryside. GM foods foisted on us by bio-agricultural industries leave unanswered questions about their long-term effects. Thousands of refugees, including a dangerous minority of terrorists and criminals, press at our borders and threaten to stretch and maybe overwhelm our national resources. Racial tension stalks our city streets. Crimes of violence abound while state surveillance of the innocent raises concerns about individual freedom. The health services are felt to be inadequate and you might just be left to die if the hospital managers deem you uneconomic or too old to treat. Computers on which we place so much reliance are prone to viruses, hackers and indeterminate faults that can bring business to a frozen halt in seconds. Commuting to work by train or plane might be the last journey you ever make. The stock markets are volatile and global economic collapse is a real possibility.

Now there are plenty of commentators, pundits and prophets offering us their analysis of the situation. But our purpose in writing this book is more urgent. People are afraid. They wonder if life will ever be safe again. What of the future? Is the end of the world imminent?

Panic lurks not far beneath the surface. In the UK the petrol crisis of 2000 brought the nation almost to a standstill as people queued, often for little more than a litre of fuel, fearful that life would grind to a halt. It was symptomatic of the anxiety that afflicts our national consciousness.

Jesus of Nazareth prophesied, 'Men will faint from terror, apprehensive of what is coming on the world' (Luke 21:26).

His prognosis is prophetically accurate and his remedy for our fears and anxieties is reliable. Drawing on the ancient wisdom of the most widely read book in the world, it is possible to understand the times, to find hope and confidence for the future, and to know what to do today. We offer the pages that follow as an attempt to explain how.

Shalom.

John Houghton
Dave Roberts

1
The Signs of the Times

'When these things begin to take place, stand up and lift up your heads, because your redemption is drawing near.' (Luke 21:28)

Many in the Arab world seriously believe that the audacious attack on the World Trade Center was perpetrated by Israel as a means of persuading the West to fight Islam and so give Israel leave to persecute the Palestinians. They say that Jews were warned to stay away from the buildings on the 11th September and that helped account for the relatively small number of casualties compared to the numbers that there might have been.

The Western governments, on the other hand, are unequivocal in their belief that the atrocity was carried out by followers of terrorist leader Osama Bin Laden, and they claim to have evidence for this.

Others, notably in the Christian community, see the issue less in political terms and more in moral and spiritual ones. Several different views emerged from America. Moral

Majority founder Jerry Falwell told broadcaster Pat Robertson, 'The abortionists have got to bear some burden for this, because God will not be mocked, and when we destroy 40 million little innocent baby lives, we make God mad. I really believe that the pagans and the abortionists, and all the feminists, and all the gays and lesbians who are actively trying to make that an alternative lifestyle, the ACLU, the People for the American Way, all of them who have tried to secularise America, I point the finger in their face, and I say, "You helped this happen."' He went on to say that such people's actions have turned God's anger on America.

Not all were so blunt, but many felt the same way. David Wilkerson, known to many as the daring young pastor of the famous *The Cross and the Switchblade* account of evangelising New York gangs, told his congregation, 'Yesterday, standing before the smouldering five-storey-high pile of rubble, I cried inwardly, "Oh Lord, if every American could stand here and behold this awful destruction, they could come to the only possible conclusion: God is warning this nation to repent."'

Chuck Colson, a politician in the Nixon administration who subsequently became a committed Christian and a highly respected figure within the American church, told the readers of *Christianity Today*:

> I approach this subject gingerly because it's easy to be misunderstood, and I try to avoid end-times prophecy that makes Christians appear irrelevant to the world. Still, the question must be asked: Can we discern God's purposes in these earth-shaking events? Might God be using these attacks as a warning of impending judgement? We must always be careful about how

> we express this to our friends. We're not blaming God for terrorist attacks. God does not create evil, but he does use it to his purposes. That's a big difference. I've been deeply burdened since September 11. I find myself at times crying for God's mercy – for myself, the church, my ministry and our country.

Tim Keller, pastor of the Manhattan-based Redeemer Presbyterian Church, offers perhaps the most reflective comment of this small survey. In a web page that advised his congregation how to respond to the questions people were asking he said:

> Our life plan may still include terrible tragedy, just as did Jesus' life plan. We learn that we cannot be sure that disasters imply divine judgement nor that prosperity implies divine approval. So how can we know whether God is displeased with America or not? The only way to know for sure is to consult the Scripture and its standards. But this does not mean we cannot 'hear God's voice' in a time of tragedy. We can. Jesus was also asked whether certain corporate and personal tragedies were 'judgements' of God. In Luke 13 he was asked if a massacre and (ironically) a falling tower were signs of God's judgement on those killed. His answer was an unequivocal 'no', but he added cryptically 'you yourselves should repent'. That fits with C. S. Lewis' famous statement that 'in prosperity God whispers to us, but in adversity he shouts at us'. God speaks to us in all troubles. So what is God saying in times of tragedy and suffering? I think the message is different depending on how touched you are by disaster.

Mega-crises raise mega-questions. Are we nearing the end of the world? What is the meaning of the current events? Is it possible to know the future? Should we change the way that we live? We need to know how to interpret the signs of our times in these apocalyptic days not only in respect of the 11th September but in the light of any other calamity that might confront us.

The end of the world

Scarcely ever has the Western world been so interested in the end of the world. Throughout all ages there have been people who believed and acted in the expectation that the world would end soon, but globalisation, mass communications and the reality of nuclear weapons of mass destruction have given the prophets of doom a whole new impetus. Apart from the nuclear threat, we have biochemical terrorism, or mutating GM crops. We might be hit by a wayward asteroid or devastated by a massive volcanic eruption that blots out the sun and destroys civilisation. Perhaps global warming will melt the polar caps and we'll all drown, or maybe holes in the ozone layer will kill us all by cosmic radiation. We might, of course, be invaded by aliens. Hollywood has done rather well out of all this, as have some religious cults.

Alarmists often have a religious predilection. Around the time of Jesus, the Essene community came into being as a purification movement to anticipate the end of the world. In our own day, cults like the Solar Temple have drawn people out of society and sometimes to their deaths because of such beliefs. Jehovah's Witnesses, while not advocating such extremes, are well known for their call to prepare for a new world.

Followers of Jesus believe that he will return and that the world as we know it will end when he does so. '*Christ has died; Christ is risen; Christ will come again.'* Jesus gave clear and specific teaching about the future of mankind and about his own return. He also told us how to behave in the light of that teaching. But that has not stopped people making it complicated. Nor has it prevented some bizarre behaviour.

In New Testament times some Christians gave up work altogether because they thought that the Second Coming was so close. Yet they still wanted feeding by those who felt differently! Paul's advice is to the point: 'If a man will not work, he shall not eat' (2 Thessalonians 3:10).

In our own day, we have had Christians so convinced that Jesus will secretly snatch them away that they have become hyperactive evangelists with no time for anything else. While their zeal is commendable, it can make it difficult for them to engage with the issues of real life. In our view, this cultural negativism has done great harm to the Christian cause, contributing significantly to its waning influence during the last century. The church urgently needs to look again at its eschatology!

Watchmen are needed in every society, prophets who will disturb our complacency and alert us to the times. However, we must beware of being blown about by every wind of doctrine, or of treating every disaster as a signal of the end. Older Christians will remind us that in the Second World War many believed that Hitler was the Beast and Mussolini was the Antichrist. Nasty as those dictators were, history ran a different course to what the pundits anticipated.

There is plenty of money to be made out of speculation. Numerous American preachers told their congregations to buy generators and to stock up with supplies in anticipation of the millennium and the collapse of global and local computer systems. Storekeepers must have loved them! Publishers know that it profits to publish a prophet, even if the supposed prophecies are complete garbage. Millions are made out of horoscopes, fortune cookies, palmistry and crystal gazing, so desperate are we to know the future. It is symptomatic of our age. As G. K. Chesterton is often quoted as saying, 'When men stop believing in God they don't believe in nothing; they believe in anything.'

Understanding the times

How then are we to evaluate our own times?

The jury will be out for many years on what the 11th September 2001 means. The consensus will be determined by who wins the subsequent war against terrorism, and how long it takes, and at what cost. Was this a judgement of God for the rapacity of American capitalism and its appalling exploitation of the world's poor? If so, then the World Trade Center was certainly a well-chosen target, a vivid prophetic symbol that you might be forgiven for thinking was a fulfilment of Revelation 18:

> Fallen! Fallen is Babylon the Great! She has become a home for demons and a haunt for every evil spirit, a haunt for every unclean and detestable bird. For all the nations have drunk the maddening wine of her adulteries. The kings of the earth committed adultery with her, and the merchants of the earth grew rich from her excessive luxuries. . . . Therefore in one day her plagues will overtake her: death, mourning and famine. She will be consumed by fire, for mighty is the Lord God who judges her.

> When the kings of the earth who committed adultery with her and shared her luxury see the smoke of her burning, they will weep and mourn over her. Terrified at her torment, they will stand far off and cry: 'Woe! Woe, O great city, O Babylon, city of power! In one hour your doom has come!' (Revelation 18:2, 3, 8–10)

Yet, with profoundest respect to the relatives and friends of those who were killed on that fateful day, we have to say that if it was an act of divine justice, it was remarkably merciful compared to the numbers of people who might have been killed. Recent earthquakes in China and Turkey have cost many more lives and produced much more misery, as have the floods in Mozambique and Bangladesh. Or what about the numbers of Iraqi conscripts killed during the Gulf War or the numbers of victims of the Hiroshima and Nagasaki bombings? The judgement of God theory seems far too simplistic.

Was it then an infidel attack against a godly nation? Large numbers of Americans are church attenders and unlike Great Britain the US government publically acknowledges God, yet few Christians would want to class it as a godly nation. The United States is a world leader in consumerism, pollution, abortion, pornography, sexual perversion, rape, murder and armed robbery. And it is precisely this godless behaviour that provokes some fundamentalist Muslims and drives them to believe that they are the instrument of Allah to purge this (as they see it) decadent Christianity from the planet. It is little use telling these people that it is secularism and not Christianity which causes this decadence; the fundamentalist mindset recognises no such entity as the secular state, or separate church. All of life is religious. Whatever else the cause, America is hardly suffering persecution for righteousness' sake.

Some people have their own personal reasons for hating America. We may never know if the now notorious Osama Bin Laden was once snubbed by an American woman or whether he is motivated simply by religious puritanism, or whether he just wants power in Saudi Arabia and perceives that America stands in his way.

That God is ultimately sovereign over all the affairs of humanity is one thing; that he gives us a frightening amount of slack is another. It took one bullet to initiate the First World War and in consequence all the other major wars of the twentieth century. God is always giving us the choice between retaliation or forgiveness; history is made by how we choose.

The United States government, along with Britain and others, has made its choice and has set out to pursue those who attacked its citizens. It is understandable; terrorism is by definition unjust since it lays on its victims the punishment for the whole perceived national guilt. It cannot be ennobled by appeals to deity or justice or politics. The terrorist is a criminal and must be brought to book. Time will tell whether America is going about it in the right or wisest manner but it is inconceivable that it would do nothing at all.

But as well as action, the events of recent times should also provoke reflection. Sooner or later the United States will want to consider why it has so many enemies and to address these matters constructively. We hope, too, that its secularists will recognise the futility of creating a society without God that is so contrary to the intents of their founding fathers and that provides so much moral ammunition for its enemies. Nor can the church consider itself exempt from renewal and reformation. The fight must go on against both fundamentalist bigotry and moral and spiritual decline. And yes, we recognise that this message needs to be heard in our own nation just as much.

True prophecy

What are the true signs of the times? We turn to Jesus of Nazareth's teaching on the last days. This is the period of time that runs from his Ascension into heaven until his return. He had this to say in answer to his disciples' questions about the fall of Jerusalem, his return, and the end of the age:

> Watch out that no-one deceives you. For many will come in my name, claiming, 'I am the Christ,' and will deceive many. You will hear of wars and rumours of wars, but see to it that you are not alarmed. Such things must happen, but the end is still to come. Nation will rise against nation, and kingdom against kingdom. There will be famines and earthquakes in various places. All these are the beginning of birth-pains. Then you will be handed over to be persecuted and put to death, and you will be hated by all nations because of me. At that time many will turn away from the faith and will betray and hate each other, and many false prophets will appear and deceive many people. Because of the increase of wickedness, the love of most will grow cold, but he who stands firm to the end will be saved. And this gospel of the kingdom will be preached in the whole world as a testimony to all nations, and then the end will come. (Matthew 24:4–14)

Sound familiar? It is exactly how the world has been since Jesus spoke these words. It is a true prophecy and we should take such words seriously instead of turning to the oddball prophecies of others, like Nostradamus, who at best have dubious reputations. What can we learn from Jesus' words?

First, that life in this God-rejecting age will always have its share of trouble but we are not to treat these troubles as signs of the end of the world. Disturbing, yes, but no cause for alarm! Indeed, the Bible promises us that the nations and the heavens themselves will be shaken so that what is unshakeable will be revealed for all to see. Followers of Jesus take times of trouble as opportunities to praise God for his quake-proof government – 'since we are receiving a kingdom that cannot be shaken, let us be thankful, and so worship God' (Hebrews 12:28). This does, naturally, raise the question as to where we have placed our own personal security.

Second, these events are the birth pangs of a new age to come. The apostle Paul picks up on Jesus' words in his letter to the Romans.

> We know that the whole creation has been groaning as in the pains of childbirth right up to the present time. Not only so, but we ourselves, who have the firstfruits of the Spirit, groan inwardly as we wait eagerly for our adoption as sons, the redemption of our bodies. (Romans 8:22–23)

Birth pangs are painful, but they are also the sign of hope. Followers of Jesus believe that every pain points forward to a day when futility will end and if, as in nature, those birth pangs grow in intensity and frequency then that merely assures us that the Lord's coming draws nearer. We are encouraged to anticipate the end of the world, not morbidly, but because it heralds the final redemption of the physical as well as the spiritual world.

Stand upright

Followers of Jesus are called to assume a unique stance. We are to build and invest in our culture as though the world will last for another thousand years; we are at the same time to live as though the Lord may return today. This means that we legitimately pursue our careers, raise our families, book our holidays, invest our money and plan for our retirement; but we do so conditionally. Rather than producing uncertainty, such a stance actually releases us from a false bondage to these expectations. If we have a light hold on them; they will not grip us.

The end of the world will not be the end of life but the end of evil; it will mark the dawning of the genuine new age of light that is characterised by unspoiled goodness. So it is not something to be feared but welcomed. In the West we grow rather too comfortable with our good life. Maybe that is why those in other nations suffering persecution and privation more readily look forward to Christ's coming.

The third point to note from Jesus' prophecy is the one clear sign that he gives concerning the end of the world: the message of the gospel, the good news of his government, will be proclaimed to all nations. It is highly possible that this will be achieved in our lifetime. By our prayers and endeavours we may hasten the time when 'the earth will be full of the knowledge of the Lord as the waters cover the sea' (Isaiah 11:9). Already the majority of the people groups in the world have in some form or other received the gospel. In excess of ten thousand of the twelve thousand people groups on the planet now have a church planting movement in their midst. Louis Bush of the AD 2000 movement estimated that eight out of ten people in the world could now have access to the whole Bible in their own language and that over 95 per cent of the world's population now has access to the good news of Jesus Christ through a portion of Scripture, radio transmission, audio recording, the *Jesus* film, or public evangelism.

We are not to detach ourselves from society like some beleaguered outpost holding out until the heavenly cavalry arrives. Instead we are called to be salt and light in our culture, purifying where we can and pointing the way to Christ. We are pilgrims but also servants to those around us, bearing witness to Jesus by our words, our works and our wonders performed in his name. Like Jesus, we are to incarnate the word of God to our colleagues, our neighbours and our families. Rather than speculating about where we are on the divine calendar we are to live lives that please God and that commend the faith. Paul reminds Titus of this:

> For the grace of God that brings salvation has appeared to all men. It teaches us to say 'No' to ungodliness and worldly passions, and to live self-controlled, upright and godly lives in this present age, while we wait for the blessed hope – the glorious appearing of our great God and Saviour, Jesus Christ, who gave himself for us to redeem us from all wickedness and to purify for himself a people that are his very own, eager to do what is good. (Titus 2:11–14)

People react in different ways during times of trouble. Ask anyone what they would do if this were the last day of their lives and you will get one of three responses. Some would immediately set to, putting their lives in order, straightening out their affairs, reconciling their relationships and making their peace with God. Others would assume a happy-go-lucky stance, blithely carrying on as usual, oblivious to any responsibility or consequence. And others would determine to indulge themselves in every possible pleasure while they could and would set out on an orgy of sex, booze, drugs and mayhem – 'eat, drink and be merry, for tomorrow we die'.

We may not know when the world will end, nor for that matter when our lives will cease, but we can choose how to live in the meantime. Psalm 90 offers us some ancient wisdom:

> The length of our days is seventy years – or eighty, if we have the strength; yet their span is but trouble and sorrow, for they quickly pass, and we fly away. Who knows the power of your anger? For your wrath is as great as the fear that is due to you. Teach us to number our days aright, that we may gain a heart of wisdom. (Psalm 90:10–12)

Prayers

The Bible teaches us that the most important thing about the future is not to speculate about it but to be prepared for it. We do that best by living worthy lives right now.

Here is some guidance. Read the following scriptures and then pray in your own words, or use the prayer that we have provided.

> Be very careful, then, how you live – not as unwise but as wise, making the most of every opportunity, because the days are evil. Therefore do not be foolish, but understand what the Lord's will is. Do not get drunk on wine, which leads to debauchery. Instead, be filled with the Spirit. Speak to one another with psalms, hymns and spiritual songs. Sing and make music in your heart to the Lord, always giving thanks to God the Father

for everything, in the name of our Lord Jesus Christ. (Ephesians 5:15–20)

Dear Lord, I honour the fact that history is in your hands and that you watch over the days of my life. I confess that I do not always use my time wisely and yet it is the most precious possession that I have. Thank you that you can teach me what is good and right. I pray that you will help me to be filled with your good Spirit, to have your song in my heart, and to be thankful in all that I think, say or do. Amen.

But do not forget this one thing, dear friends: With the Lord a day is like a thousand years, and a thousand years are like a day. The Lord is not slow in keeping his promise, as some understand slowness. He is patient with you, not wanting anyone to perish, but everyone to come to repentance. But the day of the Lord will come like a thief. The heavens will disappear with a roar; the elements will be destroyed by fire, and the earth and everything in it will be laid bare. Since everything will be destroyed in this way, what kind of people ought you to be? You ought to live holy and godly lives as you look forward to the day of God and speed its coming. That day will bring about the destruction of the heavens by fire, and the elements will melt in the heat. But in keeping with his promise we are looking forward to a new heaven and a new earth, the home of righteousness. So then, dear friends, since you are looking forward to this, make every effort to be found spotless, blameless and at peace with him. (2 Peter 3:8–14)

Lord, when I think about the end of the world it fills me with awe and I realise how small I am before your glorious majesty and power. I confess that even though you promise a better world, I am very attached to this one. Yet in my heart I know that it must one day end and I want to be prepared for that. Thank you for your patience in sparing us all this long so that we might bring our lives into line with your will. I pray that you will help me to be ready to meet you when the time comes. I recall your words to watch and pray lest we enter into temptation. In the midst of many temptations to do wrong help me to do what is right, for your name's sake. Amen.

2
Secure Foundations

> 'So do not fear, for I am with you; do not be dismayed, for I am your God. I will strengthen you and help you.' (Isaiah 41:10)

A new epidemic of fear gripped the world on the 11th September 2001. Fear of hijacking, fear of planes used as bombs. Still to come was the fear of death by post. Terrorist attacks were no longer merely news items, but were being unfolded graphically before the astounded eyes of a worldwide television audience.

While most of us faced the fear from a distance that fateful day, one man faced it head on. Todd Beamer was a passenger on United Flight 93, the plane that plunged into the ground in Somerset County, Pennsylvania. Beamer, a graduate of a Christian college and an executive in the computer industry, told the GTE telephone operator that he knew he was going to die, but that he and some other passengers were going to do something. Using their mobile phones they had heard what happened at the Pentagon and in New York.

Perhaps they hoped they could regain control of the plane and prevent a similar carnage.

Todd, it seemed, was not a man who would retreat from a difficult situation. In his in-tray at home he kept a quotation from Theodore Roosevelt: 'The credit belongs to the man who is actually in the arena, who strives valiantly: who knows the great enthusiasms, the great devotions, and spends himself in a worthy cause.'

He asked the operator to phone his wife and children for him and then they said the 23rd Psalm and the Lord's Prayer together. He left the line open, and turned to some other men sitting in the back of the plane and said, 'Let's roll.'

We may never know what happened, but hundreds, perhaps thousands, of lives were saved as a result of their action.

His wife, Lisa Beamer, writing in *A Reason for Hope* (Crossway), speaks of both pain and a godly passion. 'Although I suffer indescribable human pain, the knowledge of God's eternal good coming from these events is an unwavering anchor for me and will be for our boys someday as well.'

She urges her readers to discover Christian hope. 'I pray too, as you face the challenges of each day, that you are never without hope, through faith that is founded in the sovereign, loving God. . . . May you be strengthened in hope and courage to dare greatly for God, leaving lukewarm faith behind.'

One of the most forceful challenges to us following the 11th September was the question of what we would do if terrorism came to our town. Should the people of the church run for shelter in other places, or should we stay to help those who can't help themselves?

The answers are found in the life of the Man who could have returned to his place alongside the Father, but chose to remain on earth to help those who couldn't help themselves. What can we discover from the life of Christ about why the innocent suffer? What does his life say to us about our eternal security? How can we respond to fear as he did? How can he help us in the everyday realities of a sometimes cruel world?

The greatest hero

Tales of heroism impress all of us, especially when the heroes are ordinary mortals. Death itself comes to everyone, but none of us wants to die prematurely, violently or unexpectedly. Nor do we wish our death, or the deaths of our loved ones, to be pointless. Acts of bravery help to ease the sense of futility that we otherwise might feel. The quiet courage of the child dying of cancer, the passer-by who is murdered while intervening to save someone from assault, the person who plunges into a freezing torrent to save a drowning child, the lone hero who stands before an advancing tank – these people act as beacons of hope in an uncertain world. Jesus spoke truly when he said, 'Greater love has no-one than this, that one lay down his life for his friends' (John 15:13).

Jesus was no theorist; he was to take the hero's path himself, and to a greater extremity than anyone else. One epoch-making day, in the thirtieth year of his life, he stepped from behind his carpenter's bench and descended the hill country of Nazareth to be baptised in the River Jordan. God – not some deaf, dumb, dead delusion of human invention, but the living Creator – spoke, declaring Jesus to be his incarnate Image, his true Son.

That event inaugurated three astonishing years of preaching, teaching, healing, exorcism and miracles that were destined to change the course of human history and that today, more than ever, define the future for each one of us.

Those three years culminated in the cruel and unjust execution of the finest man who ever walked the earth. Yet, in the space of three days, he was miraculously raised to life again, appearing to his bemused disciples, and giving full credence to his claim: 'I am the resurrection and the life. He who believes in me will live, even though he dies' (John 11:25).

The sacrificial death and resurrection of Jesus lie at the heart of the Christian message of hope for humanity. The first beneficiary was a convicted criminal, crucified next to Jesus, who acknowledged his own guilt and then asked for mercy from the one he knew was innocent. Jesus promised him paradise that same day. Death would not be the end; soon the hell of crucifixion would give way to a state of timeless refreshment in the presence of Jesus.

The dying thief was the first; since then countless millions have believed and so will millions more – all over the world, from every race and in every generation, until the end of time.

Eternal life now

But eternal life is much more than the guarantee of a blissful afterlife. It is a present reality. Followers of Jesus know right now a quality of radiant spirituality that springs from an inner personal relationship with Jesus himself. It's like being in love, having a best friend, being welcomed home. Sometimes it's like relaxing to cool music, sometimes like cheering the winning goal. It's running through the breakers on the shore, gazing long at wistful vistas, gasping in wonderment at starbursts, catching tantalising glimpses of angels – all this and more, and always with a profound sense of life-giving and life-affirming companionship.

This fellowship with Christ is profoundly rooted in the meaning and purpose of his death and resurrection.

There are cultures where men become blood brothers by cutting themselves and rubbing the open wounds together to mingle their blood – a decidedly dangerous practice nowadays! Yet the spiritual relationship between Jesus and his followers is similar. When he was executed, Jesus took our 'bad blood' into himself, and he has given us his 'good blood'. The New Testament theologian, Paul, says, 'God made him who had no sin to be sin for us, so that in him we might become the righteousness of God' (2 Corinthians 5:21). This is an astonishing exchange. Jesus loved us so much that he bore the curse of our death so that we might receive the blessing of his life. We might expect that he would sacrifice his life for someone worthy enough, but Jesus died for us unworthy people who showed little sign that we would ever change our ways. 'God demonstrates his own love for us in this: While we were still sinners, Christ died for us' (Romans 5:8).

The life of Jesus is pure and holy. When we put our faith in him, Jesus actually breaks the grip that our rebellious and self-centred state of being has on our lives and we receive a transfusion of his good life into us that begins marvellously to change the way that we behave.

Faith in Christ also changes our status; from now on we will be assessed before God not on our failings but on Christ's obedience. Our relationship with God changes from being that of guilty moral criminals in his sight to being that of much-loved children. 'Therefore, since we have been justified through faith, we have peace with God through our Lord Jesus Christ' (Romans 5:1).

Paul goes on to speak about our certainty of being in the presence of God when we die and of the way that God saturates our inner being with his love by the gift of his Holy Spirit. Little wonder then at the profound joy so characteristic of followers of Jesus, even though life may at times be very hard. It led the apostle to pen the eloquent words:

> Who shall separate us from the love of Christ? Shall trouble or hardship or persecution or famine or nakedness or danger or sword. . . . No, in all these things we are more than conquerors through him who loved us. For I am convinced that neither death nor life, neither angels nor demons, neither the present nor the future, nor any powers, neither height nor depth, nor anything else in all creation, will be able to separate us from the love of God that is in Christ Jesus our Lord. (Romans 8:35, 37–39).

Death transformed

The gift of eternal life transforms how we view death. Many people say that they are not afraid of death, but put them into a life-threatening situation and they will behave as though they were afraid of death! Let's not kid ourselves: unless we are in a psychologically morbid condition we want to stay alive and will do all we can to avoid dying. The survival instinct that is produced in times of danger – the familiar 'freeze, fight or flight' response – is simply another way of saying that we all fear death.

It is the fear of death that makes us fight our corner, protect our property, guard our health, promote our ego, defend our territory, destroy our enemies. It can also sometimes render us powerless – speak to anyone who has ever suffered panic attacks or lost the will to live because of the death of a loved one or grave news of cancer. Then that fear can seem really evil, quite demonic in fact.

Jesus came to destroy the devil's power and to deliver us from our lifelong bondage to this fear of death (Hebrews 2:14–15). He, by his own death and resurrection, drew the sting from the scorpion and guaranteed that one day even the bodies of his followers would be raised from the dead and transformed into a supra-physical state; that is, with enhanced physical powers beyond even the most far-flung imaginings of our sci-fi writers. The nearest we can get to understanding this is to observe the transformation that took place when Jesus was raised from the dead. He was no ghost and yet he could materialise in different places at will. He could eat a solid breakfast, show a doubting Thomas his wounds, and ascend to heaven in gravity-defying splendour. It's just a tantalising hint of the future!

Of all the uncertainties and possibilities about the future one matter is absolutcly certain. Jesus of Nazareth is coming back again, and there will be a world for him to come back to. All the hundreds of prophecies concerning Jesus' first coming have been fulfilled to the letter; everything he said about life on earth until the present has proved to be true; there is no reason to doubt that the many prophecies, and his own promises to return, will prove equally trustworthy. Here is just one, given by the angels who attended his Ascension: 'This same Jesus, who has been taken from you into heaven, will come back in the same way you have seen him go into heaven' (Acts 1:11). When he does so, the bodies of his followers who have died will be raised again to life and all those who are currently alive will undergo the most amazing metamorphosis ever seen – a mass ascension to meet their returning Lord in the sky! Every true believer can live, and die, in this expectation. The Apostles' Creed declares, 'I believe in . . . the resurrection of the body,' and the Nicene Creed affirms, 'We look for the resurrection of the dead, and the life of the world to come.' Early church defender of the faith, Tertullian, writes, 'The confidence of Christians is the resurrection of the dead; believing this we live' (*De Resurrectione Carnis*).

In the course of a number of years as a church leader, John has conducted many Christian funerals. He always views them as seed planting occasions – *'in the sure and certain hope of the resurrection of the body, through our Lord Jesus Christ'*.

> Listen, I tell you a mystery: We will not all sleep, but we will all be changed – in a flash, in the twinkling of an eye, at the last trumpet. For the trumpet will sound, the dead will be raised imperishable, and we will be changed. For the perishable must clothe itself with the imperishable, and the mortal with immortality. (1 Corinthians 15:51–53)

Forget just snuffing it. Forget reincarnation. This is what will really happen!

The presence in the midst of pain

Christianity isn't a happy-go-lucky religion. Followers of Jesus experience the same trials of life as anyone else; they feel the same emotions, too. Sometimes they are confused and on the brink of despair; on occasions they are afraid. Pain hurts. Two months after the attack on the World Trade Center many innocent Pakistani Christians were martyred for their faith during Sunday worship. We feel shock, anger, hurt and grief at the news. Yet God does not remove his presence, nor our Christian hope. The poet David wrote, 'Even though I walk through the valley of the shadow of death, I will fear no evil, for you are with me; your rod and your staff, they comfort me' (Psalm 23:4).

On occasions the divine protection is remarkable. Isaiah the prophet spoke God's words to a frightened people:

> Fear not, for I have redeemed you; I have called you by name; you are mine. When you pass through the waters, I will be with you; and when you pass through the rivers, they will not sweep over you. When you walk through the fire, you will not be burned; the flames will not set you ablaze. (Isaiah 43:1b, 2)

This was famously the experience of Shadrach, Meshach and Abednego during the time of the Jewish exile, as recorded by Daniel the prophet. The Babylonian monarch Nebuchadnezzar had built a 90-foot-high golden idol and ordered everyone to bow down to it on pain of live cremation. These men, being good Jews, refused and were arrested. Their bold defence went like this:

> If we are thrown into the blazing furnace, the God we serve is able to save us from it, and he will rescue us from your hand, O king. But even if he does not, we want you to know, O king, that we will not serve your gods or worship the image of gold you have set up. (Daniel 3:17)

As good as his word, the king had them thrown into his blast furnace only to see God incarnate himself in their midst and keep them from harm to such an extent that they were not even singed by the heat. The remarkable event brought about the conversion of the Babylonian king.

Job, in a time of sickness, financial ruin and family tragedy, entrusts his future to God and anticipates the resurrection we spoke of earlier:

> I know that my Redeemer lives, and that in the end he will stand upon the earth. And after my skin has been destroyed, yet in my flesh I will see God; I myself will see him with my own eyes. (Job 19:25)

Handel based his famous aria on these words when he composed *The Messiah.*

Job, after learning one or two important lessons about himself and his God, recovered. We know this doesn't always happen. Christian believers die, sometimes because of illness or accident, sometimes because of persecution, sometimes even of old age! Yet all can say, 'My times are in your hands' (Psalm 31:15). As mentally sound people we pray, as Jesus taught us, 'Lead us not into temptation, but deliver us from evil.' And we have a lot of sympathy with a man named Jabez who sensibly prayed, 'Let your hand be with me, and keep me from harm so that I will be free from pain' (1 Chronicles 4:10). Yet, having done all this, our security is not in the fervour of our prayers; it is in Jesus himself. When he appeared in a vision to John, the oldest of his disciples, he said, 'Do not be afraid. I am the First and the Last. I am the Living One; I was dead, and behold I am alive for ever and ever! And I hold the keys of death and Hades' (Revelation 1:17–18). Ultimately, no follower of Jesus dies by accident or at the devil's hand – nor do they die alone.

Whatever comes upon the world, however bleak the outlook, we can all enter this certainty. Jesus promised, 'I will be with you always, to the very end of the age' (Matthew 28:20). Life can be a perilous journey, and filled with uncertainties at times. This would seem a good moment to reflect on the grounds of your inner security and to ask yourself about your relationship with Jesus. God grants us eternal life; it is a free and unconditional offer – and this life is found in his Son. 'He who has the Son has life; he who does not have the Son of God does not have life' (1 John 5:12). It's as simple as that.

> For God so loved the world that he gave his one and only Son, that whoever believes in him shall not perish but have eternal life. For God did not send his Son into the world to condemn the world, but to save the world through him. (John 3:16)

Prayers

As we respond to turmoil in the world we need four things: a relationship with God through Christ, trust in his compassion for us, perseverance in difficult times, and wisdom for the everyday decisions of life. Take time to read the scriptures below, reflect on them and then pray in response to God's promises.

Salvation

> If we confess our sins, he is faithful and just and will forgive us our sins and purify us from all unrighteousness. (1 John 1:9)

If you confess with your mouth, 'Jesus is Lord,' and believe in your heart that God raised him from the dead, you will be saved. (Romans 10:9)

Trust

My times are in your hands. (Psalm 31:15)

So do not fear, for I am with you; do not be dismayed, for I am your God. I will strengthen you and help you; I will uphold you with my righteous right hand. (Isaiah 41:10)

Patience and perseverance

For our light and momentary troubles are achieving for us an eternal glory that far outweighs them all. So we fix our eyes not on what is seen, but on what is unseen. For what is seen is temporary, but what is unseen is eternal. (2 Corinthians 4:17–18)

As you know, we consider blessed those who have persevered. You have heard of Job's perseverance and have seen what the Lord finally brought about. The Lord is full of compassion and mercy. (James 5:11)

Wisdom

If any of you lacks wisdom, he should ask God, who gives generously to all without finding fault, and it will be given to him. (James 1:5).

The wisdom that comes from heaven is first of all pure; then peace-loving, considerate, submissive, full of mercy and good fruit, impartial and sincere. (James 3:17)

Dear Lord, in these anxious and perplexing days I need to know you. I realise that I don't deserve to, but I thank you that you are full of love for those who seek your help. Please forgive the things that need forgiving in my life. I put my trust in you for my future and I pray for your strength to help me do what pleases you. Grant me courage and wisdom so that I may be at peace and that I may bring your peace to others. I ask this in your precious name. Amen.

3

Comforting the Confused and Hurt

'There is no fear in love. But perfect love drives out fear, because fear has to do with punishment. The one who fears is not made perfect in love.' (1 John 4:18)

A friend of ours was working in a supermarket in the days following the 11th September. He overheard a woman in the queue phone someone on her mobile phone. 'I just wanted to call and say I love you,' she said. This was not the flirtatious call you might make to the love of your life. Her body language suggested that it was simply a close friend. The friend seems to have enquired as to why she should call on a mobile in the middle of the day. The lady in the queue explained her sense of bewilderment at the events of previous days, and the feeling that things might change, and that the people who mattered to her should know it.

Another friend phoned Dave's wife, Sharon. The lady, not a regular churchgoer, simply asked if she could talk about the events of the previous week. She had friends in the community, but for a more reflective conversation she turned to someone with a faith and hope she had come to respect. We've spent time studying the Scriptures with her as she has joined a midweek meeting in our home.

For some there has been just an inner shift, a loss of optimism about world affairs turning out all right. Others have felt a new pessimism that expresses itself in a caution about flying, or an increased interest in personal security. For yet others there is a great sadness, a sense of melancholy as events in another nation cascade into the emotional, financial and personal safety aspects of our lives.

Two months after the event, on Remembrance Sunday, John spoke over coffee to the husband of one of our church members, himself not a regular attender. 'I felt I had to come today,' he said. 'It just seemed important on this particular Sunday, what with everything that is happening around us.' He is a college lecturer with numerous Muslim students in his classes, many of whom wondered if they would be allowed to stay in Britain. His other students had expressed little interest in the events. Perhaps they were not yet fully aware of life and were concentrating on studies in the hope that nothing would touch them personally.

How can we respond to the hurt, confusion and worry that this tragedy has brought, and that further events may bring?

Age of uncertainty

We live in an age of uncertainty. Gone are the days when life followed its daily, weekly, monthly, seasonal and yearly cycles and it was legitimate to talk predictably of the seven ages of man. Gone, too, are settled communities where people spent their lives in close contact with their friends and neighbours, where fathers apprenticed sons and a job was for life. The mills of God may grind slow and fine but the mills of men today are geared for maximum efficiency and throughput as we race through the technological revolution in search of some undefined paradise beyond.

Settled ways of life tend to have settled sets of beliefs. Our fast-changing world has yet to find a set of beliefs with which to handle change. We have fragmented in both belief and commitment; consensus is now no more than a temporary expedient indulged in by self-contained individuals for personal gain. Loyalty travels no further than the current economic contract. We live where we do while the job lasts; our commitment to local institutions is haphazard; even sexual relationships have a sell-by date. Should our lifestyle be threatened, then it is everyone for themselves. Any beliefs we have centre upon the satisfaction of our ego.

This fragmented and individualised culture is very threatening to some. They like neither the changes nor the rate of change. Alvin Toffler called it 'future shock' and it lies at the heart of many of the anxieties and neuroses in our society. None of this is helped by terrorist attacks that further threaten our security, making listening to the news an exercise in depression alleviated only by the final light anecdote included to encourage us to come back for more of the same in an hour's time.

It is more than terrorism and war, of course. Every disaster is reported by our global media coverage and many of these have ramifications for our own security. Or, at least, they appear to; for part of the catch is this power of the media to bring news as it is happening right into our homes, thereby implying that we are at some sort of personal risk. John will confess to looking out of the window to see what else was happening in the local skies as he watched the events of the 11th September unfold three thousand miles away in Washington!

From time to time, these threats become realities for the individuals concerned. A gunman goes wild in a local school, one train collides with another, a hijacked plane is flown into an office block, a bomb explodes in a pub. There are real victims on our doorstep, and distraught friends and relatives. Meanwhile, the subconscious anxiety and stress level of the national consciousness rises a little more and life is a little less stable. Veteran BBC reporter, Jeremy Bowen, after being mugged in a south London street near his home, wrote, 'I am sure the police are doing their best. But a society in which people are scared to walk home at night is not healthy' (*The Mail on Sunday*, 28 October 2001).

All this is leading many people today to lose faith in the old certainties of science, reason and progress. The modern world, for all its spectacular technological achievements, has not brought peace on earth, nor has it satisfied the longing of the human heart for meaning. Many are exploring the old paths of spirituality once again. Gone are the days when materialism was seen as the be-all and end-all of life.

This exploration may take people in some weird and unhelpful directions but it has created a new climate of openness that means it is once more legitimate to talk about spiritual experience, to admit that you pray and meditate, to speak of spiritual healing and encounters with the divine. In this postmodern climate it is no longer politically correct to dismiss or criticise the Christian faith, since it too must be deemed a valid expression of spirituality. Followers of Jesus, so used to being marginalised, need to take the opportunity to express their spirituality without shame. However, let us do so with grace and not with the harsh dogmatism that has caused so much offence in the past. The postmodernist begins with respect for the spectrum of belief; he does not have any absolutes, so starting in with absolute answers to questions not yet explored is simply going to close the door to further discussion. What will impress much more is a life-style of grace, one that is free from religious legalism and that radiates the winsome love of God to those around.

Mercy ministry

It is often said that compassion knows no creed; certainly compassion is at the heart of the Christian creed. God himself is merciful and compassionate. He does not readily judge.

> The Lord is compassionate and gracious, slow to anger, abounding in love. He will not always accuse, nor will he harbour his anger for ever; he does not treat us as our sins deserve or repay us according to our iniquities. For as high as the heavens are above the earth, so great is his love for those who fear him; as far as the east is from the west, so far has he removed our transgressions from us. As a father has compassion on his children, so the Lord has compassion on those who fear him; for he knows how we are formed, he remembers that we are dust. (Psalm 103:8–14)

Nowhere is this more clearly expressed than in the sacrificial death of his own Son on our behalf.

Since God is like that, so are all his true children. The two greatest commandments are: love God and love your neighbour. That love and compassion begin at the very simplest level of showing kindness to those around us. John and his wife, Jan, have a friend who during the petrol crisis joined a late night queue for fuel; then, seeing that she had half a tank full, said to herself, 'Other people here must be in greater need than I am. I can wait until another time.' She left the queue to make room for others. Naive? Maybe. But if everyone had behaved with the same thoughtfulness there would have been no queues, no panic buying, and no real shortages.

Opportunities for showing mercy abound in everyday life, from helping someone who is stuck on a job to visiting the sick, from befriending a refugee to baby-sitting for a single parent. Our church provided daily meals recently for a family in which a teenage daughter was dying of an incurable brain tumour; it was at least one load off the shoulders of her distressed parents.

Compassion can also include bringing words of comfort, consolation and encouragement, especially to those who are traumatised, grieving or just plain worried. King Solomon understood that words were more powerful than sticks or stones:

> Reckless words pierce like a sword, but the tongue of the wise brings healing. . . . An anxious heart weighs a man down, but a kind word cheers him up. . . . Pleasant words are a honeycomb, sweet to the soul and healing to the bones. (Proverbs 12:18, 25; 16:24)

If you want to put this to the test, just remember what it feels like when someone says, 'You look awful today!' It doesn't exactly improve your outlook if you are already under the weather. How much better when someone compliments you on looking slimmer, or approves a new hairstyle, or simply thanks you for being so pleasant. The

American 'Have a nice day' sounds corny to British ears but it's a lot better than the alternative. Many south Germans still greet one another with 'Grosse Gott' – God is great. Maybe a few more 'God bless you's wouldn't go amiss in our society.

Soul healing

The word 'psychiatry' means literally 'soul healing'; it is a pity the word has been restricted in use to a particular branch of the modern medical profession. Christian pastors have been practising psychiatry with brilliant results for centuries! With all due respect to the modern profession, what a lot of people need is simply someone who will listen to their anxieties and offer them some words of encouragement. Soul healing is much needed in these days of confusion and despair.

Jesus announced his ministry with words from the prophet Isaiah:

> The Spirit of the Lord is on me, because he has anointed me to preach good news to the poor. He has sent me to proclaim freedom for the prisoners and recovery of sight for the blind, to release the oppressed, to proclaim the year of the Lord's favour. (Luke 4:18–19)

The Christian gospel is all about making people whole. It is not for hypocrites or the self-righteous; they will never see their need of help until it is too late. It is for all honest men and women who recognise that they have human frailties, inner anxieties, and the need to make sense of life. To all such Jesus' words have a universal appeal:

> Come to me, all you who are weary and burdened, and I will give you rest. Take my yoke upon you and learn from me, for I am gentle and humble in heart, and you will find rest for your souls. For my yoke is easy and my burden is light. (Matthew 11:28–30)

This is not about dry religion; it is about entering a partnership with Jesus. He does not add to our burdens; rather, in companionship with him we experience spiritual release and come to a place of profound inner stillness. This is his encouraging promise: 'Peace I leave with you; my peace I give you. I do not give to you as the world gives. Do not let your hearts be troubled and do not be afraid' (John 14:27).

Many people are searching for such peace today. The followers of Jesus have the best news possible to offer the world in a time of trouble.

This peace is deeper than simply a relief from anxiety. It deals with the fundamental alienation between God and ourselves brought about by our self-centred rebellion against him. In the story of the Garden of Eden, Adam and Eve made the choice to be godlike without God. Their descendants have, within limits, done the same. But we cannot deal with the evils of the human heart. Those evils are sometimes blatant, as in terrorist attacks or child abuse; but they are there in all of us and honest people recognise the reality of what they sometimes call their 'dark side'.

What makes Jesus unique is that he was conceived by the Holy Spirit and was consequently born without a dark side. He lived a life in perfect harmony with himself and with God and at the end offered that life freely for us. His death took on the power of our dark side and all that lies behind it, and overcame it. Jesus was the Victor over evil; he took the punishment we should have received as a consequence of our evil and made it possible for us to be reconciled to God through simple faith in him.

So begins, in those who believe, a transforming process anticipated by the prophet Ezekiel:

> I will sprinkle clean water on you, and you will be clean; I will cleanse you from all your impurities and from all your idols. I will give you a new heart and put a new spirit in you; I will remove from you your heart of stone and give you a heart of flesh. And I will put my Spirit in you and move you to follow my decrees and be careful to keep my laws. (Ezekiel 36:25–27)

Beginning with the Jewish people who believed, this simple message and the outpouring of the Holy Spirit that accompanied it soon began to spread to all nations of the earth, so that today followers of Jesus are found in almost every culture and region on the planet.

If you have experienced the soul healing, the *shalom*, brought about through this good news then you are in a good position to help others. This does not mean that you have to give every person that you meet the entire Bible! However, we can all pray that we will have a word in season for those whose path parallels our own. We can ask God to give us words of wisdom and share a little of our own experience of transformation. We can tell them a bit about Jesus and encourage people to pray to him.

If you have not yet begun that soul healing process, then this might be a good time to start. Here are some more prayers that you may like to use.

Prayers

Using the Hebrew word for wholeness, *shalom*, God promises peace to those who trust him: 'You will keep in perfect peace him whose mind is steadfast, because he trusts in you. Trust in the Lord for ever, for the Lord, the Lord, is the Rock eternal' (Isaiah 26:3–4).

Here is a simple prayer of faith for personal wholeness, first used by the prophet Jeremiah: 'Heal me, O Lord, and I shall be healed; save me and I shall be saved, for you are the one I praise' (Jeremiah 17:14). You might like to pray it too.

God grants us this wholeness so that we can pass it on to others also:

> Praise be to the God and Father of our Lord Jesus Christ, the Father of compassion and the God of all comfort, who comforts us in all our troubles, so that we can comfort those in any trouble with the comfort we ourselves have received from God. (2 Corinthians 1:3–4)

This comfort may be ministered by our words but also by our actions:

> This is how we know what love is: Jesus Christ laid down his life for us. And we ought to lay down our lives for our brothers. If anyone has material possessions and sees his brother in need but has no pity on him, how can the love of God be in him? Dear children, let us not love with words or tongue but with actions and in truth. (1 John 3:16–18)

> Lord, make me an instrument of your peace;
> where there is hatred, let me sow love;
> when there is injury, pardon;

where there is doubt, faith;
where there is despair, hope;
where there is darkness, light;
and where there is sadness, joy.
Grant that I may not so much seek
to be consoled as to console;
to be understood, as to understand,
to be loved as to love;
for it is in giving that we receive,
it is in pardoning that we are pardoned,
and it is in dying [to ourselves] that we
are born to eternal life. Amen.

(A prayer of Francis of Assisi)

Lord, I know I cannot do everything, but help me do something. The needs of the world overwhelm me, but the needs of my neighbours invite me. I have too little time, too little money and too little skill to offer but I put what I do have into your hands to make them count more than they otherwise would. May I receive your comfort and so become the instrument of your comforting love and mercy to those you place across my daily path. For your name's sake. Amen.

4
Blessed Are the Peacemakers

'Peacemakers who sow in peace raise a harvest of righteousness.' (James 3:18)

I (Dave) sat watching a Christian TV show. The host, a very famous figure, suggested that part of the response to the World Trade Center atrocities should be to 'carpet bomb' parts of Afghanistan. One of his guests, a million-selling author, affirmed loudly, 'That's the word of the Lord!' Angry as I was over the atrocities of the week before, I felt more anger welling up at this armchair spiritual blasphemy and hastily switched the television off.

'Islam is a religion based on vengeance.' These were the words of a friend of mine, recently recounting a tape he had heard. He visits Arab lands and is not known to be a bigot.

By contrast, a pastor from San Diego told us how her church members sought to actively show love to the local Arab and Muslim population by offering to go shopping with Arab women, housebound for days and weeks following the 11th September attacks, and fearful of personal attack if they ventured out. She was deeply troubled, none the less; a visiting Arab Christian pastor had outlined in graphic detail the sinister intentions of Islam worldwide.

That some sections of this worldwide religion are violent towards other faiths is hard to refute. An estimated two million Christians and animists have died in the Sudan at the hands of the Muslim government, according to a 6th November 2001 *Washington Post* article. The article reflects the view of the Washington-based Center for Religious Freedom when it states: 'In terms of draconian government restrictions, Saudi Arabia, Nigeria, Afghanistan and Turkmenistan are the most severe.' An estimated 5,000 people have died in Indonesia since 1999 at the hands of the Muslim militia and as many as 400,000 have been made refugees. At the time of writing over 350 people are estimated to have died at the hands of Muslim extremists in Nigeria since the 11th September.

However, to condemn all of Islam because of this would be comparable to condemning Protestantism because of the activities of paramilitary groups in Ulster. Other voices, therefore, sound a caution about holding a one-dimensional view of Islam. Lynn Green, a leading figure in the biggest missionary agency in the world (Youth With A Mission), was one of those who organised the Reconciliation Walk, retracing the steps of the crusaders 900 years before. On their way from Germany to Jerusalem they talked with many Muslims. 'The majority of Muslims that I have come to know in recent years are decent, God-fearing people who will deeply identify with our grief in these days,' he said.

Some commentators pin most of the blame on evil leaders – with some justification Saddam Hussein, Osama Bin Laden and others have spent the past decades painting an evil caricature of America and the West. That caricature has not been drawn from scratch. Some of the policies and behaviour of our nations had painted their own ugly picture long before the distortionists began their work.

Lynn recounts a conversation with a thoughtful Shi'ite Muslim leader, who said: 'Evil and power-hungry people often use religion as a tool to manipulate the masses.' Lynn reminds those reading his newsletter: 'It is hard to make an airtight case for Islam being any more violent than the fundamentalist movements of other religions.'

He concludes:

> There could never be justification for the acts of terror we have witnessed in recent days, but this is such an important time for us to listen. The guilty must be identified and brought to justice, but we must take great care that we do not further damage those who are the neighbours of the guilty.

Loving our enemies includes trying to understand why they are our enemies. Much of the Islamic revulsion against Christianity can be traced back to those medieval crusades, during which the unholy alliance of the cross and the sword brought untold suffering to the Muslim population. Over 2,000 Christians from 27 countries participated in that YWAM-sponsored Reconciliation Walk. They retraced the old crusade routes wearing T-shirts with the words 'I apologise' in Arabic or Hebrew and offering apologies for the gross injustices blasphemously done in the name of the Prince of Peace. The Roman Catholic church has likewise expressed its regrets for the crusades. Many Muslims, including religious leaders, have been profoundly moved by the gesture.

One of the first stops for the walk was a Turkish mosque in Cologne. An apology was read, which reflected, 'Where they were motivated by hatred and prejudice we offer love and brotherhood. Jesus the Messiah came to give life. Forgive us for allowing his name to be associated with death. We renounce greed, hatred and fear and condemn all violence done in the name of Jesus Christ.' Following this, the Turkish imam spoke. 'When I heard the nature of your message, I was astonished and filled with hope,' he said. Later on, he told a walker that the Muslim community was beginning to examine their sins against Christians and Jews and said that the Walk might spur them on.

Some people have a natural gift of peacemaking. As with all good gifts it comes from God, but it carries a price. Peacemakers are often the most despised of people, called variously appeasers, traitors, betrayers of the struggle, cowardly, weak, compromisers, two-faced. Jesus said that under his government they would be called sons of God (Matthew 5:9).

The desire for revenge, for retaliation, is rooted deeply in the human psyche and in some people and nations it becomes a pathological condition, as in Northern Ireland or in the Balkans, reproducing bitterness and violence generation after generation. It is an attitude that demonises our supposed enemies *en masse* with little thought for the individual, and creates the mentality that says the only good Catholic is a dead Catholic. For Catholic insert *Protestant*, or *Black*, or *White*, or *Jew* – or *Muslim*. Whatever the target of this hatred may be, callousness, bigotry and ignorance lie at its root.

The Muslims are the latest target of bigotry and ignorance. It is understandable; the atrocities against the Americans and others are done in the name of Islam. The Taliban is revealed as a medieval, totalitarian, religious police bringing oppression to the people of Afghanistan and harbouring an enemy of the predominantly Christian West. Iraq, Libya and many other Muslim nations have behaved aggressively against the West, too, and resurgent Islam persecutes Christians in many less developed countries. In parts of Indonesia the Christian population faces virtual genocide, yet George W. Bush and Tony Blair raise no voice on their behalf.

How then are we to respond to Muslims and Arabs in our neighbourhood and around the world? We suggest a threefold response.

Love your enemies

Even if Islam in its current form proves to be an enemy of the Christian faith we are called by Jesus to love our enemies: 'Love your enemies and pray for those who persecute you, that you may be sons of your Father in heaven' (Matthew 5:44–45). Christ died for our enemies as well as for us. He died for the bigoted Jewish establishment and for the Roman provincial government that between them crucified him. That is why he prayed, 'Father, forgive them, for they do not know what they are doing' (Luke 23:34). Jesus also died for the Muslims.

In the midst of a kill-or-be-killed world, true followers of Jesus, while legitimately defending themselves and their loved ones against unprovoked attack, will speak with a prophetic voice, calling for our enemies to be won over by acts of kindness. The thirteenth chapter of Paul's letter to the Romans grants to the state the role of maintaining justice; it is preceded by a call for God's people to fulfil a higher role:

> Do not repay anyone evil for evil. Be careful to do what is right in the eyes of everybody. If it is possible, as far as it depends on you, live at peace with everyone. Do not take revenge, my friends, but leave room for God's wrath, for it is written: 'It is mine to avenge; I will repay,' says the Lord. On the contrary: 'If your enemy is hungry, feed him; if he is thirsty, give him something to drink. In doing this, you will heap burning coals on his head.' Do not be overcome by evil, but overcome evil with good. (Romans 12:17–21)

No one pretends that this is always easy, but the alternative is to continue with endless, unresolvable conflict and slaughter.

Belief and behaviour

Loving our enemies does not mean agreeing with everything they say. For political reasons Prime Minister Blair and President Bush want to play down the differences between Christianity and Islam. The Prince of Wales has been quoted as saying he would prefer to be the defender of 'faiths' rather than the defender of *the* faith – that is, the Christian faith. His dalliances with other religions are well-documented. These attitudes reflect the prevailing unthinking establishment mantra that 'all religions lead to the same God' – a statement that is insulting to both Muslims and Christians.

There are major differences between the Islamic deity and the God of the Bible. Allah is a singularity; Yahweh is a monoplurality, three-in-one, a Trinity. Allah is a lawgiver; Yahweh is a merciful lawgiver who sacrificed his own Son to deliver us from the consequences of the law. Acceptance with Allah comes through obedience to Qur'anic law; acceptance with Yahweh comes through faith in Jesus Christ. While many in Judaism, Islam and Christianity regard much of the scriptural law as positive wisdom for everyday living, only Christianity proposes that salvation is not found in a legalistic observance of that law but in the grace of God poured out through the sacrificial death of Jesus. In Islamic theology Jesus is only a prophet; in Christianity he is the eternal Word made flesh, the Son of the living God.

That does not imply that there is no common ground for dialogue. On the contrary. In an extended plea for a more thoughtful response to our Islamic neighbours, Christine A. Mallouhi, while recognising the differences, asks the readers of *Waging Peace on Islam* (Monarch) to take an approach more reminiscent of Paul's conduct at Mars Hill in Acts 17, where he affirmed rather than condemned some of the tenets of the local religion, in order to point the way to Christ.

She notes in the process that her Muslim friends were amazed to hear the concept of forgiveness expressed in the Lord's Prayer. 'In a culture built on retaliation . . . An eye for an eye, a tooth for a tooth . . . free and necessary forgiveness is revolutionary.' She adds, 'The Christian belief that our sins are forgiven through Christ here and now is difficult for Muslims, as they believe the outcome cannot be known until the day of judgement.'

We must tread carefully when talking of the beliefs and intentions of Islam worldwide. The *Columbia Encyclopaedia* says this of the Sunnis:

> Sunni Islam should be understood as an umbrella identity, grouping close to 90% of the approximately one billion Muslims,

> stretching geographically from the Indonesian islands to the African steppes, through the Indian subcontinent, central Asia, and the Arab world, and ideologically from ecstatic Sufism to the puritanic literalism of the Wahhabis and Salafias, through scholasticism and secularism. The scholastic formulation, the most constant expression of Sunni Islam throughout its history and geographic span, proposes the relation of the human being with the Divine as essentially individual, with no intermediaries. In actual practice, however, religious scholars (ulama), together with mystic shaykhs, pious persons, and popular saints (awliya), are often recognised as enjoying a religious authority of varying degrees.

This is not far removed in structure to Protestantism and its regard for the Bible, though in this case it is the Qur'an. The Shi'ite faith, strong in Iran, is more akin to Catholicism, with only the key figures descended from Ali, the son-in-law of Muhammad, able to speak with authority from God.

The Wahhabi sect is strong in many of the nations pursuing the most militant Islamic application of the law to the whole population. Osama Bin Laden finds his own spiritual roots in this group, which has been heavily funded in recent times by its Saudi adherents.

The *Columbia Encyclopaedia* describes the Wahhabis as follows:

> It was founded by Mohammed ibn Abd al-Wahab (c.1703–1791), who taught that all accretions to Islam after the 3d cent. of the Muslim era – i.e., after c.950 – were spurious and must be expunged. This view, involving essentially a purification of the Sunni sect, regarded the veneration of saints, ostentation in worship, and luxurious living as the chief evils. Accordingly, Wahhabi mosques are simple and without minarets, and the

adherents dress plainly and do not smoke tobacco or hashish. Driven from Medina for his preaching, the founder of the Wahhabi sect went into the NE Nejd and converted the Saud tribe. The Saudi sheikh, convinced that it was his religious mission to wage holy war (jihad) against all other forms of Islam, began the conquest of his neighbours in c.1763.

Words and deeds

Whatever the system of beliefs, faith must be judged by conduct. When a professing Christian exhibits aggression against others he is denying the faith. The same has to be true for the Muslim; if Muslims murder ordinary citizens through acts of terrorism then we have every right to question the validity of their personal religious commitment. Criminal acts committed by Christian or Muslim must be subject to the due processes of the law. If Osama Bin Laden is behind the recent outrages, then he should be brought to justice. That is part of the role of the state. Christians are committed to personal forgiveness but that does not mean that we are indifferent to justice.

An interviewee on a recent BBC *Songs of Praise* programme told how she was caught in an IRA terrorist bombing. She was badly injured but survived and married, only to discover when she and her husband wanted children that the bomb blast had rendered her infertile. Worse, the hospital had known this but had not informed her until she had sought fertility treatment. Her testimony of suffering was moving; even more so was her struggle to reach the place where she could, through the grace of Christ, forgive those who had injured her. When at last she did so, she experienced a wonderful inner release. This Christian lady is a fine testimony to Christ's transforming power and grace. That does not stop those of us who hear the story from holding the IRA culpable for its crimes, nor the hospital administration for its unethical conduct.

Spectrums of belief

It is easy to demonise everyone who is different from us, especially if some of them prove to be our enemies. As men and women of peace we do not want to be tarred with the same brush as the militants of Northern Ireland or Serbia. Similarly, we must treat Muslims with respect. There is as wide a spectrum of belief and behaviour among cultural Muslims as there is among cultural Christians. Many in both religions are nominal and their faith in practice consists of no more than a folk belief in their deity coupled with a general desire for decency and a quiet life. It probably also includes a moderate celebration of the annual faith festivals. Such are many of the Sunnis.

There are others who, while active practitioners of their faith, are none the less moderate in their attitudes towards non-believers, preferring to build bridges rather than barricades, to win by personal example and personal testimony rather than by coercion. Most of these see the futility of violence and so choose a non-violent manner of life, if not outright pacifism. It is possible to exercise a principled tolerance that, while disagreeing fundamentally with the faith of others and seeking for their conversion, can still work for peaceful co-existence. In such a climate constructive discussion is possible and areas of mutual concern can be addressed to the benefit of all. It is a position we personally advocate.

Christine Mallouhi comments on the crusader mentality among Christians and encourages the readers of *Waging Peace on Islam* to consider:

> How can we continually paint Muslims as hostile spiritual enemies with whom we are engaged in the greatest battle of our century, and then be willing to go to our Muslim neighbours and share Christ's love with them? . . . people rarely respond positively to those waging war on them.

Unfortunately, in the religious world as in the secular, there are always fanatics to be found – people who are prepared to advocate and use physical force to impose their beliefs on others. Their strident voices get into the media and cause grave offence, be they Christian fundamentalists or Muslim. Legitimising violence to further the Christian faith is contrary to Scripture. We fight on a different front. Paul writes:

> For though we live in the world, we do not wage war as the world does. The weapons we fight with are not the weapons of the world. On the contrary, they have divine power to demolish strongholds. (2 Corinthians 10:3–4)

For this reason we choose to distance ourselves from the heresy of militant Christian fundamentalism. The same must go for Islam. The Wahhabi sect is violently anti-West and anti-Christian. It is surely abhorrent to all right thinking people, including the majority of Muslims.

Let us do good

Many refugees currently seeking to enter the United Kingdom are Muslims. The policy of allowing them in is controversial because of the limited resources of these overcrowded islands. Yet Jesus assessed the reality of our faith in him by our attitudes to those without a home: 'I was a refugee and you took me in.' Many Christians have opened their doors and their hearts to genuine asylum seekers, with churches and individuals involved in projects in a number of places around the British Isles. They offer friendship, clothing, advice and English language classes. Nick Reynolds of New Addington Community Church said of the motivation behind their projects, 'Our motivation . . . must be that God has asked us to. Our role is not to make judgements but to extend mercy and demonstrate the unconditional love of Jesus.'

The parable of the Good Samaritan reminds us that going to meetings, being concerned about our own purity, and performing religious duties at the expense of the needy is to fail to obey the second great commandment, which is to love our neighbour as ourselves. Our neighbour is whoever we stumble across in need during the course of our life. Jesus makes the point more pertinent by using a Samaritan to care for a Jew, the equivalent of a Palestinian assisting a modern-day Israeli – or an Afghan helping an American.

Because the Christian faith recognises no racial, sexual or class barriers it should be instinctive for us to judge people by their need and by nothing else. But that can be costly. Years ago, a Christian doctor, Sheila Cassidy, treated a wounded rebel in Chile. She was arrested and tortured by the state as a consequence, but she did the right thing and the publicity surrounding her sufferings helped bring an end to that corrupt regime.

There is more than one kind of courage in the world. Many think only of the soldier on the battlefield and find it hard to consider the merciful as anything other than spineless wimps. Yet it is not the case, as witness the many martyrs for the Christian faith who bear no weapons, but stand simply for the truth and serve others, even their enemies, with the love of Christ. We need many who will offer an alternative to the violence of this fallen world.

Muslims for Jesus

Since Christ died for the Muslim population as well as the rest, Muslims have the right to hear the message of salvation. Yet we must present it sensitively. Merely condemning someone else's beliefs can only provoke dismay or anger. There is little point in winning an argument if in the process you lose the person.

Our starting point must be friendship and a recognition that many Muslims come from a different ethnic background from ourselves. That background defines their culture and we must beware of suggesting that in order to become followers of Jesus they must abandon their culture in favour of ours. This will prove highly offensive to many devout Muslims, simply because they abhor the low moral standards of the West and will interpret us as meaning that they must abandon their own high standards.

The amazing thing about the Christian faith is that it does not impose an alien culture but redeems the inherited culture of the converts. This is something that we need to recognise – not only with Muslims but with Jews and others also. The Council of Jerusalem, recorded in Acts 15, released Gentile converts from the need to assume Jewish culture and allowed the gospel to spread like wildfire across the Roman Empire. Who knows what we might see when we begin to respect legitimate cultural differences? It might also assist us in our quest for church unity, for the vast majority of issues that divide Christians from one another have nothing to do with foundational doctrine; they are simply a matter of in-house cultural traditions.

When we do get to communicating the gospel with those of a different religion from ourselves we need to do so graciously, listening, explaining, discussing, seeking to understand, rather than forcing our arguments upon our listeners. We also need to do so in the context of hospitality, including food and drink.

Jesus engaged in dialogue with the woman at the well, crossing the cultural, racial, religious, moral and sexual divides. He did so with grace and clarity in such a manner that this woman became an avid follower and an evangelist among her own culture. The barriers that divide the human race so tragically are broken down when people are truly introduced to Christ.

Prayers

In a stinging rebuke on his people for religious piety that lacked any real care for those around them, Isaiah the prophet cries:

> Stop bringing meaningless offerings! Your incense is detestable to me. New Moons, Sabbaths and convocations – I cannot bear your evil assemblies. Your New Moon festivals and your appointed feasts my soul hates. They have become a burden to me; I am weary of bearing them. When you spread out your hands in prayer, I will hide my eyes from you; even if you offer many prayers, I will not listen. Your hands are full of blood;

> wash and make yourselves clean. Take your evil deeds out of my sight! Stop doing wrong, learn to do right! Seek justice, encourage the oppressed. Defend the cause of the fatherless, plead the case of the widow. (Isaiah 1:13–17)

All true religion, faith and belief will be judged by this threefold standard: 'He has showed you, O man, what is good. And what does the Lord require of you? To act justly and to love mercy and to walk humbly with your God' (Micah 6:8).

Jesus put it like this:

> Love your enemies, do good to those who hate you, bless those who curse you, pray for those who ill-treat you. If someone strikes you on one cheek, turn to him the other also. If someone takes your cloak, do not stop him from taking your tunic. Give to everyone who asks you, and if anyone takes what belongs to you, do not demand it back. Do to others as you would have them do to you. (Luke 6:27–31)

Paul agrees:

> Do not repay anyone evil for evil. Be careful to do what is right in the eyes of everybody. If it is possible, as far as it depends on you, live at peace with everyone. Do not take revenge, my friends, but leave room for God's wrath, for it is written: 'It is mine to avenge; I will repay,' says the Lord. On the contrary: 'If your enemy is hungry, feed him; if he is thirsty, give him something to drink. In doing this, you will heap burning coals on his head.' Do not be overcome by evil, but overcome evil with good. (Romans 12:17–21)

Lord, this is a vindictive world and I look with grief at the cycles of vengeance and hatred that I see among nations and also within families. It is even worse when it is perpetuated in the name of God. Keep my spirit free from it. I want to be a peacemaker and I ask you, the Prince of Peace, to fill me with your kindness for others. Make me a bridge-builder, a healer of hatreds, an instrument of mercy. For your name's sake. Amen.

Bless, O Lord, all those who seek peace and pursue it. Give your help to all true diplomats and envoys, to all restrainers of evil, to the rebuilders of communities shattered by violence. Guard them from corruption and despair. Grant them harvests of righteousness from the seeds of peace that they have sown. Amen.

5
A People of Prayer

'When I am afraid, I will trust in you.' (Psalm 56:3)

As we recorded earlier, along with many other churches throughout the world we called a prayer meeting on the evening of the 11th September. We did so out of a sense that we needed to be together for a few hours and help each other understand what had just happened, but also in response to Paul's injunction to Timothy:

> I urge, then, first of all, that requests, prayers, intercession and thanksgiving be made for everyone – for kings and all those in authority, that we may live peaceful and quiet lives in all godliness and holiness. This is good, and pleases God our Saviour, who wants all men to be saved and to come to a knowledge of the truth. (1 Timothy 2:1–4)

People say in resignation, 'We can only pray.' But is this the one thing left to do when all the real options are exhausted, or is it the most important thing we can do? In

The Passing of Arthur, Alfred Lord Tennyson wrote, 'More things are wrought by prayer than this world dreams of.' We are quite certain that our prayers, and the prayers of millions of other Christians, acted as a divine restraint on the more aggressive figures in the United States government who might have been tempted to make a swift and possibly brutal retaliation for the atrocities of the 11th September. It also released us from a sense of impotence and anxiety.

We prayed for six matters and distributed our prayer list to the entire congregation on Sunday the 16th. As we have sought to research how other churches responded we found many similar lists posted on church web sites on the 11th and 12th September. The areas covered were as follows:

- Prayer for the families of the bereaved and all who sought to help them.
- Prayer for wisdom for governments and leaders (1 Timothy 2:1–2).
- Prayer for all those experiencing fear and vulnerability, especially children.
- Prayer for Arabs and Muslims in our home town. While not sharing their beliefs we recognised that many of them were as appalled as we were. We sought to guard ourselves against prejudice (Luke 10:25–37).
- Prayer for the church to provide practical, moral and spiritual leadership. The events of that day were a wake-up call to the church and our nation. Our man-made securities were shaken (Revelation 18:1–20).
- Prayer for the 'peace of Jerusalem', recognising that the conflicts in and around Israel were in some way linked to the events in New York.

As we seek to live faithful lives in the midst of crisis, what hope do prayers such as these bring? What lies at the root of the prayer impulse that many feel? How does prayer change us? And what does God do in response to our prayer?

Everyone prays

Prayer is a universal human activity. It may be misdirected in its object sometimes but just about everybody prays at some time during their lives, and a vast number of people who do not attend church none the less pray regularly. We spoke with a lady recently whose sister was murdered by a fanatical religious cult. The woman in question finds it very difficult to associate with any cohesive group of people as a result, but she prays daily and wants her family to pray together also.

Most of us pray, not because we have a religious bent, but because we recognise how vulnerable we are in this world. Life is tenacious but it is also fragile. We delight to see the unbounded energy of children but we know, too, that their lives can be blotted out in an instant by disease, by road accident, or by abduction. John and his wife recall being on a French west coast beach known for its dangerous currents and undertows. A child had gone missing and the distraught parents were calling his name. Although there were many thousands on the beach a hush of apprehension fell across the crowds; many would have been quietly praying for the child's safety.

We may see people suffering terrible pain or hardship. Some of these may be our nearest and dearest. Other images may come through our media. Such distress is beyond our capacity to help. So we pray.

We view with alarm the follies of fanatics and political leaders who jeopardise our lives, often for their own short-term agendas. As the current threat of global war grows, we pray.

Strangely, most of us do not question if, why or when God will answer our prayers; we just know that it is the right thing to do. This implicit spiritual response reminds us that we were made to connect with God. The apostle Paul, addressing the crowds on Mars Hill, put it like this:

> From one man he made every nation of men, that they should inhabit the whole earth; and he determined the times set for them and the exact places where they should live. God did this so that men would seek him and perhaps reach out for him and find him, though he is not far from each one of us. 'For in him we live and move and have our being.' (Acts 17:26–28)

God is always closer than we think – 'a very present help in time of trouble'.

Spiritual growth

Prayer is an expression of creaturely dependence, but it also provides an opportunity for spiritual growth. By talking with God we learn to listen, to reflect and to consider. At such times as these God is apt to drop into our hearts the word of wisdom that we need for our circumstances. In our busy, chattering world we need more praying and less discussing, and more listening in our praying. We will then experience an amazing peace.

> Do not be anxious about anything, but in everything, by prayer and petition, with thanksgiving, present your requests to God. And the peace of God, which transcends all understanding, will

guard your hearts and your minds in Christ Jesus. (Philippians 4:6–7)

We will also come to a better consensus as to the right course of action.

The apostle Peter wrote his first letter to people who were facing a time of great trial. He gave this advice: 'Cast all your anxiety on him because he cares for you' (1 Peter 5:7). It is simple advice but a reminder of the character of God. He really is merciful and kind. 'As a father has compassion on his children, so the Lord has compassion on those who fear him; for he knows how we are formed, he remembers that we are dust' (Psalm 103:13–14).

It is only as we pray that we really discover the truth about God's character. Faith is not a spectator sport; it can only be understood by engagement on the field. We have questions about why the innocent suffer, why moral decline is so rampant, and about why religion causes so much trouble. These will never be resolved by theorising and philosophising about God. All we do is reveal our ignorance of his character and ways of working. By spending time in prayer, by reading the Bible, we begin to educate ourselves properly. We will come up with surprisingly good answers to these seemingly unanswerable questions. There is little point in passing those answers on to those who are not prepared to pray, however, because they will not be able to receive them. It's a bit like trying to explain Fermat's last theorem to someone unwilling to learn their multiplication tables.

Of course, we may become the answers to our own prayers. Sometimes the very act of prayer provides us with the needed motivation to do what deep down we know the will of God to be. In prayer we walk through the possible scenarios and outcomes – a spiritual dummy run, if you like – and gain the clarity and courage that frees us to act, even if it is sometimes costly to do so. 'Give me time to pray about it' is not avoiding a decision; it is an essential part of making the right decision and acting upon it with conviction.

We see this most clearly when Jesus prayed in the Garden of Gethsemane just prior to his arrest and crucifixion. He had long known that his destiny was to lay down his life for others. He was no coward; nor did he question the rightness of God's will for his life. Yet the thought of taking the evil of the world on his own shoulders, the decision to let his pure soul be contaminated beyond measure, to become sin for us and as a consequence to endure separation from God – that was truly awful to contemplate. Little wonder, then, that Jesus prayed, 'My Father, if it is possible, may this cup be taken from me' (Matthew 26:39). Three times Jesus prayed this prayer and on each occasion he concluded, 'Yet not as I will, but as you will.' Having settled the issue he rose with calm resolve to face his ordeal and so bring salvation to the world.

Judgement mode, mercy mode

Does prayer really change the course of history? There are certainly many instances of this phenomenon recorded in the Bible. For example, King Hezekiah, living in Jerusalem at the time of Isaiah the prophet, was facing the might of the invincible Assyrian army. All the land in the path of this cruel and ruthless invader had fallen and now they were at the gates of Jerusalem. Hezekiah took the letter conveying the terms of surrender required by the Assyrians, 'Then he went up to the temple of the Lord and spread it out before the Lord. And Hezekiah prayed to the Lord' (Isaiah 37:14–15). As a result, God remarkably delivered the city, and the Assyrian army, struck down with a sudden and devastating plague, retreated back to their homeland leaving Judah in peace.

The Bible suggests that the will of God is not a fixed, deterministic programme. Rather, in his absolute sovereignty, God has elected as an act of outrageous grace and love to interact with those made in his image. If that were not so, prayer would be philosophically pointless, a mere charade. As it is, God writes 'ifs' into even his direst threats of judgement. Thus to King Solomon he says,

> When I shut up the heavens so that there is no rain, or command locusts to devour the land or send a plague among my people, if my people, who are called by my name, will humble themselves and pray and seek my face and turn from their wicked ways, then will I hear from heaven and will forgive their sin and will heal their land. (2 Chronicles 7:13–14)

God will change his stated intent in the light of people's change of heart even when dealing with pagan nations. This is the message of the book of Jonah. The prophet, after an unnecessarily complicated sea voyage, proclaims imminent judgement and doom over the inhabitants of Nineveh. The population, from the king downwards, repents. God spares the city. Jonah is thoroughly peeved at the outcome because he has not yet understood that God far prefers to act in mercy mode than in judgement mode.

The early church theologian, Origen, wrote, 'War occurs when the prayers of Christians fail.' He was right. War is an unqualified evil. It is a time when God lifts his hand of protection, allows the demons their way, and brings judgement upon the nations concerned. It is never to be welcomed. We are to pray for peace.

Abraham, foreseeing the judgement of Sodom and Gomorrah, interceded for God to spare the righteous, negotiating the terms:

> Then Abraham approached him and said: 'Will you sweep away the righteous with the wicked? What if there are fifty righteous people in the city? Will you really sweep it away and not spare the place for the sake of the fifty righteous people in it? Far be it from you to do such a thing – to kill the righteous with the wicked, treating the righteous and the wicked alike. Far be it from you! Will not the Judge of all the earth do right?' (Genesis 18:23, 25)

Lot and his family were spared as a result of Abraham's intercession.

The sins of the West cry out for judgement. We are provoking God to anger by our wilful rejection of his will for our lives. Instead of honouring God, we blaspheme his name and despise even the Ten Commandments in our arrogance. Only a minority are prepared to worship God and to give him thanks for his blessings. Sexually we are promiscuous and adultery is rife; our rampant consumerism exploits the poor in other lands. We abort our children, we blaspheme the name of God, we believe more easily in witchcraft than in divine power. We lie and cheat and steal, with many, including those in high places, believing that the only real crime is being found out. Violence is on our streets and in our homes. Drunkenness and substance abuse are at an all-time high. Yet the gospel is being proclaimed among high and low and there are large numbers of people who truly love God's name in our nations. We should pray for mercy and work to spread the good news of Jesus' salvation before it is too late. For if we do fall into judgement mode it is the nation as a whole that is judged and the individuals, whatever the rights and wrongs of their own lives, get swept along with it. This is something we need to learn afresh, as our brothers and sisters in the less developed world have already learned. The time and passion we are prepared to devote to prayer leaves us falling dismally short.

Things are changing. Houses of prayer, lighthouses of prayer, prayerwalking, prayer centres and many more initiatives are springing up in many places to replace the dwindling church prayer meetings of a previous generation. Prayer forms an integral part of the programme for most cell church groups. We are encouraged by the 24/7 prayer movement that seeks to establish non-stop round-the-clock praying. It is time to seek the Lord.

Revisit your prayer life

Times of trouble invite us to review the condition of our prayer lives.

The starting point is to 'pray without ceasing'; that is, to cultivate such a sense of the presence of God that we find it the most natural thing in the world to discuss the matters of the moment with him.

However, we all benefit from specific times of quiet when we can devote ourselves to prayer. This may take place in a church building or cathedral, or on a park bench, or walking alone. It is easy for our minds to wander at such times, especially once we have finished praying for our loved ones and for our immediate needs. One of the best ways of preventing this is to use passages of Scripture, especially the Psalms, to focus our thoughts and then to pray those passages back to God. This both enlarges the range of our prayers and extends our understanding of God's will and purpose.

We may also find that prayers written by others help us to focus our thoughts and desires, whether these be drawn from the great liturgical traditions or from the writings of those noted for their devotional lives. You may find it helpful to light a candle or use some other symbol as a means of expressing your heartfelt determination and yearning when you pray. This long tradition is being revived in all manner of new contexts today.

The other prayer context that we can all benefit from is praying with a small group of trusted people. The past 50 years have seen a phenomenal growth in home groups of one sort or another. All of them allow for times of shared prayer. Others meet in small prayer triplets specifically to pray. In the home group to which we belong it is normal to pray for friends, neighbours and relatives as well as for our personal needs. We are also learning how to pray for the nations and for all those in positions of authority. We recommend that you find such a group if you have not done so already.

Here are some prayer ideas that you may wish to use.

24/7 prayer

This simply means prayer being offered to God 24 hours a day, 7 days a week. This is not as daunting as it sounds. Those who take on a one-hour shift with twelve prayer suggestions to assist them will find that the time flies by. You can find out more at www.24-7prayer.com. Here you will also find a wealth of information on how you can make a highly creative but low-tech prayer room.

Prayer couplets and triplets

Groups of two or three people meet at a convenient time once or twice a month to pray and share for a maximum of one hour. It pleases God and does those praying a world of good – not least because it gives a structure to an expression of friendship and spirituality. This sense of relational strength is vital as society continues to absorb the reality of a new era of conflict and disruption.

Fresh Prayer

Prayer liturgies can give direction to the individual and to corporate prayer in church but can be time-consuming to prepare for already busy people. The Fresh Prayer resource will be helpful to you, giving both topical and neighbourhood prayer ideas rooted in a 'praying the word' approach. Visit www.waymakers.org to register for their monthly email prayer outline. You might also like to check out their existing resource for those experiencing fear (based on Psalm 34) and those in a time of crisis (based on Psalm 95).

Prayer aids

It's always better to pray because you feel inspired or desperate – not because you feel obligated. There are many books on prayer that may give you that inspiration. We would especially recommend *Every Prayer in the Bible* by Larry Richards (Nelson). Its helpful index will assist you to pray, and to help others to pray, during times of crisis and change.

Lord, have mercy on us and teach us your ways. Bring peace to our land and keep us from disaster. We need your protection and your mercy; in wrath remember mercy, we pray. I also ask you to teach me how to pray better in the midst of my busy life, so that I may be led by your will and not just by my own anxious agendas. For the sake of your glory. Amen.

6
Leadership in Our Communities

> 'Do not be afraid; you will not suffer shame. Do not fear disgrace; you will not be humiliated.' (Isaiah 54:4)

The reaction of the Christian church to the crisis of the 11th September 2001 was swift and varied. For the New York churches the needs to be met were very practical, but for churches around the world it was a time of great challenge, as church attendance doubled in many places. Months after the crisis the well-known Anglican landmark church in London, St Paul's Cathedral, still attracted 200 extra people a week. The spiritually absent seemed to be returning to the fold, looking to find direction in a time of dislocation and despair.

For the Brooklyn Tabernacle church the needs were clear. As people streamed away from the Ground Zero World Trade Center site, the church set up tables with water and cold rags so that dust-covered people could clean up a little and begin to regain their composure. They allowed people to use the phone and simply held other shaking distraught people and quietly prayed for them.

Methodist ministers William Shillady and Bryan Hooper opened their church, donned their clerical robes and stood outside the church, ready to pray. A steady stream of people entered the church, with up to 300 people taking the chance to stop, pray and reflect. Another church opened its doors, provided lunch, and gave one sore and blistered businesswoman a new pair of shoes. It was by no means an easy task. The Revd James Korper, pastor of a Manhattan church, told a Methodist news service, 'The biggest challenge for me was to stop crying long enough to pray.'

In the ensuing weeks churches took supplies to the Ground Zero area, and dozens of chaplains sought to assist those working there. Other churches responded to the longer-term needs of New York citizens and to those of the people around the world shocked by the day's events.

Redeemer Presbyterian pastor Tim Keller and his team immediately posted advice on their website for the hundreds of New York parents in their church. The advice came from others, but Redeemer delivered it to those in need. They urged parents to give their children extra time, assure them that they would protect them, and also to monitor their media viewing. Elsewhere, they urged parents to communicate the reality of evil to their children, but remind them also of God's sovereignty and goodness.

Keller's initial email to church members urged them to pray and to visit the church website to discover how they could give practical aid. He didn't speak until he had had time to reflect, saying, 'Words fail me right now. It's really too horrible for words.'

On the 14th September he tackled the tough questions. How can you trust God after this kind of event? Is this a judgement from God? How can the Christian community avoid a vengeful mindset? He tackled many of the themes this book addresses.

In the midst of crisis the church in New York provided a place of physical and emotional comfort. It urged people to think, not merely react, and offered practical advice and biblical insight.

Hope springs from the feeling that one is not alone in the midst of surprise, shock and terror. Hope doesn't infect a community merely because one or two individuals think positive thoughts. It happens when a community of faith is both eloquent and practical, praying and feeding people, showing hospitality and helping others to reflect on God and Jesus.

But perhaps we don't see the church in our nation as a credible carrier of hope. Perhaps we believe that we can't catch the ear of our communities again or even give leadership. We are presented with the question: 'If we faced a crisis in our town would our church be any earthly use?'

The church has not gone away

We live in a supposedly post-Christian age. At least, that is what the intelligentsia who dictate our culture like to tell us. In reality however the Christian faith provides the mainstream energy, creativity and economic growth of a great variety of emerging cultures across the world, offering as it does the worldview, inspiration and sense of meaning that people need for these things to happen. It also creates the sense of community that means people can work together. It did this once in the West and laid the foundation for our modern world. However, notably in the United Kingdom, the church has been marginalised and dismissed as a formative influence, and we have paid the price for that in the fragmentation, cynicism and spiritual despair that today lies at the heart of the British psyche.

Not that the church has gone away, of course. We do more voluntary work than any other society on earth and in Britain alone our contribution to society is worth billions. We considered just a few examples from our home town. There are at least three community centres staffed by Christians, one serving as many as 1,000 people a week. The churches run numerous mother and toddler clubs. Significant quantities of low cost housing are provided by the Christian-inspired Shaftesbury Society. There is an innovative 'save sex for marriage' programme called Wise Up in local schools and after-school clubs. Several long-term, viable youth clubs and children's clubs are staffed and funded by the churches throughout the town. We have a project of retraining for the workplace underway as well as aid to the homeless, young people in need and those suffering from addictions. People in residential care homes are regularly visited by teams of people drawn from the local churches. There are many more examples besides – and this is typical of the community involvement of Christians all across the country.

People have lost a sense of belonging. True, there are many who find solace and fellowship in a voluntary organisation, sports club, pub or social club, but these organisations seldom offer moral or spiritual leadership or inspiration to change society. All of them tend to draw people of a particular type, and a clubbiness develops that excludes those who don't quite fit.

Only the church of Jesus Christ possesses the infrastructure, the passion, the motivation, the universality, the goodwill and the resources to provide for the community as a whole and for its moral and spiritual well-being and growth.

In his book *Bowling Alone* Robert D. Putnam looks at civic life through the eyes of a sociologist. The title comes from his observation that whereas people once went tenpin bowling in groups, such is the fragmentation that now many choose to go alone.

He tells his readers, 'Religiously involved people seem simply to know more people. Regular church attendees reported talking with 40% more people in the course of the day.' He says this spills over into charitable giving and volunteering. 'About 75–80% of church members give to charity, as compared to 50–60% of non-members, and 50–60% of church members volunteer while only 30–35% of non-members do.' Putnam tells us that 60% of American churches (more if you concentrate on the larger ones) contribute to social service, community development or neighbourhood organising projects. Putnam's book is popular with policy makers in the UK and may explain the interest from all political parties in the Faithworks initiative, sponsored by the Oasis Trust. This project seeks to ensure a 'level playing field' for all church-based projects in their dealings with local and national government.

New models of church

The lack of this 'level playing field' meant that many churches began to withdraw into themselves in the latter half of the twentieth century. As churches retreated to the realm of personal belief and devotion, many lost adherents and closed down; others just closed their doors and became ghettoised groups meeting in their holy barns but having little impact on the world around.

Not all of us were content with this scenario and there is

emerging a vibrant, new version of church that takes as its starting point the presence of believers in the field of everyday human relationships. This is the church as an incarnational missionary community in which all the members understand themselves to be full-time lay chaplains in their homes, their workplaces and their leisure haunts. We take seriously the call to be salt and light wherever we are, twenty-four hours a day, seven days a week. Our task is not to grasp power but to influence those in power – the business, educational, political and community leaders – to act in a godly manner for the well-being and improvement of society. It is to provide the mainspring spiritual, creative and moral energy that will make this possible. We need to pray, to educate and to engage with ordinary people so that they might discover what Jesus meant when he said, 'I have come that they may have life, and have it to the full' (John 10:10).

We want to take seriously the parable of the sheep and the goats, recorded in Matthew 25:31–46, which teaches us that real faith is much more than orthodox beliefs or a decision recorded at some point in our personal history. Instead, it is something evidenced by our redemptive engagement with the needs of others. This is what James meant when he wrote:

> What good is it, my brothers, if a man claims to have faith but has no deeds? Can such faith save him? Suppose a brother or sister is without clothes and daily food. If one of you says to him, 'Go, I wish you well; keep warm and well fed,' but does nothing about his physical needs, what good is it? In the same way, faith by itself, if it is not accompanied by action, is dead. But someone will say, 'You have faith; I have deeds.' Show me your faith without deeds, and I will show you my faith by what I do. (James 2:14–18)

When Jesus fed the five thousand he demonstrated the fullness of the gospel both by meeting the evident physical needs of the crowds through performing a miracle, and by pointing the way to himself as the Bread of Life. This was his consistent manner of bringing the word of life to people. Thus we find him preaching, but also amid the crowds, in homes, pubs and markets, eating and drinking, sharing hospitality, vulnerable to humanity, and bringing good news to the poor. He built bridges by his participation in the mundane things of life so that the profound things would be heard from a friend not a distant cleric or aloof believer.

Leading the field

Churches can be effective as incarnational missionary communities only if they engage with the culture and the people in their locality. Church leaders have become very good at producing in-house programmes for the benefit of their members. Now they are having to become good at understanding the needs and aspirations, the hopes and fears, the values and beliefs, of those who live in the community around them. This requires a great deal of research and involvement on the part of the whole church and not just its leadership.

What would happen in a time of crisis, if, heaven forbid, it happened on your patch? It's not that improbable. Floods or extreme weather could impact your town. Britain is long overdue for a mainland strong earthquake. What if your area was hit by sustained public unrest or a financial collapse that caused widespread need and social disruption? In our interconnected world it only takes one major institution to be affected for our societies to experience major chaos. Unlikely as many of these things seem they are not implausible, as the South of England experienced one year ago when the rain never seemed to cease and the waters rose to flood many low-lying communities.

Would we know what to do? How quickly could we contact all the members of the local churches to mobilise them to prayer and action? How well are we integrated with the other care providers in our community? Have we built good relationships with the local schools, hospitals, Chambers of Commerce, councillors, police and emergency services? Are we so engaged with the people in our parish in a personal and repeated manner that they would automatically think of us as a prime resource in a time of trouble? Are the local authorities aware of what contribution our congregations and buildings might make in the event of a disaster because we have, as community representatives, sought consultation in the local emergency planning meetings?

We should not delay until such time as we are in extremis; our divine mandate is to ensure that every person in our parish has a full working understanding of the Christian gospel and of the redemptive contribution of the church, irrespective of whether or not we face a crisis. This is really about restoring conversation with our neighbourhoods. It is to do with building trust and co-operation in place of suspicion and standoffishness. It is about letting the good news of Jesus Christ be good news.

Part of the price society pays for dismissing the Christian faith is the loss of moral and spiritual leadership in favour of political expediency, spin-doctored deception and market manipulation by advertisers. Not surprisingly, party politics is dying as fewer and fewer people feel it is worth bothering to vote. The present government received no positive mandate from the majority of the population and is only in power by default as a consequence of the electoral system. People no longer trust nor look to the government for leadership; merely for protection and welfare services.

The moral and spiritual vacuum which is left invites leadership. If the church does not provide it then sooner or later others will. This might be only isolated opportunists who use people for their own ends. But it might be drug barons or an emergent dictatorial government. If people cannot find spiritual leadership through the church then they will turn elsewhere. It is time for the church to arise with a new confidence in the deposit of faith and love and hope that God has bestowed upon her.

'Perfect love drives out fear,' wrote John the apostle. Paul writes to an anxious Timothy to remind him 'to fan into flame the gift of God, which is in you through the laying on of my hands. For God did not give us a spirit of timidity, but a spirit of power, of love and of self-discipline. So do not be ashamed to testify about our Lord' (2 Timothy 1:6–8). There are many in our society who feel intimidated by the events all around them, whether it be the international crisis or the fear of mugging, or just the inability to cope with the pace of change. They desperately need the power of God to give them strength, and the love of God to comfort their hearts, and the self-discipline of the Holy Spirit to keep them from panic. Christ has anointed his church in all her diverse manifestations to minister these graces to a needy world. We have no need to be ashamed of this message; never was it more needed. Jesus said, 'I have told you these things, so that in me you may have peace. In this world you will have trouble. But take heart! I have overcome the world' (John

16:33). It is a hope that all may rediscover in an age of crisis.

When the followers of Jesus pray, 'Your kingdom come; your will be done on earth as it is in heaven,' they are praying for a better form of government and they have in mind the prophecy concerning the coming of Christ:

> Every warrior's boot used in battle and every garment rolled in blood will be destined for burning, will be fuel for the fire. For to us a child is born, to us a son is given, and the government will be on his shoulders. And he will be called Wonderful Counsellor, Mighty God, Everlasting Father, Prince of Peace. Of the increase of his government and peace there will be no end. He will reign on David's throne and over his kingdom, establishing and upholding it with justice and righteousness from that time on and for ever. The zeal of the Lord Almighty will accomplish this. (Isaiah 9:5–7)

It anticipates a time when God's peace will come to this world and 'they will beat their swords into ploughshares, and their spears into pruning hooks' (Micah 4:3).

Wherever Jesus is allowed to reign there is peace – within the individual heart, or over a nation, or over the whole world. Sadly we do not yet see the world under his reign of peace, but we trust that you will find this *shalom* of God in your own heart and community as you rediscover Christian hope in an age of crisis.

Prayers

As we go into a needy, anxious world and seek to be salt and light in our neighbourhoods the prayer known as St Patrick's Breastplate captures our desire:

Christ behind and before me,
Christ beneath and above me,
Christ with me and within me,
Christ around and about me,
Christ on my left and my right,
Christ when I rise in the morning,
Christ when I lie down at night,
Christ in each heart that thinks of me,
Christ in each mouth that speaks of me,
Christ in each eye that sees me,
Christ in each ear that hears me.

Prayer while you're there

Select some streets in your area, including those that have shops, businesses, churches and schools. Take time to walk the area praying prayers of hope based on Jeremiah 32:17: 'Ah, Sovereign Lord, you have made the heavens and the earth by your great power and outstretched arm. Nothing is too hard for you.'

Lord Jesus, this is where I belong. Help me see this area as you do with all its beauty and all its brokenness. Help me to love the people here in your name. Help the churches here to spread your fame by their gracious words and practical deeds. Help us to be bridge-builders so that, whether a crisis is personal or touches the whole community, we will be found where people need comfort and peace and shelter from their anxieties. May your goodness be present here to bring healing and restoration to all who need it. Amen.

The Prayer Principles *series*

When I Can't Pray by Rob Frost

Praying isn't always easy. There is much in life to throw us off course and keep us from developing regular communication with God. Rob Frost provides food for thought and prayer for up to four weeks of daily meditations. The result is a celebration of the most rewarding relationship we can have.

Learning the Joy of Prayer by Larry Lea

Praying to the Sovereign Lord of the universe is our duty – a privilege, even. But can regular prayer be a time of great *joy* as well? Larry Lea guides us through the Lord's Prayer, as we rediscover what it means to see 'his kingdom come' in our lives.

Prayers Women Pray by Quin Sherrer

This book was written with busy people in mind – to help you focus on the things you'd like to discuss with God. It covers twelve key areas of life – including important occasions, tough times, and reaching out to friends and neighbours.

Renewing Your Prayer Life by Sue Barnett

Prayer is about relationships, not rules. Rather than giving a string of formulas for more effective praying, Sue Barnett focuses our attention on the One who both inspires and receives prayer.